AF416259

Hoosier WordArt:
Finicky Kitten's
Book of Rhymes

Finicky Kitten loves to write
her poems in rhyme with great delight.
Within these pages you will find
rhymed poems, each one of a kind.

Mary A. Couch

Copyright © 2022 by Mary A. Couch

All rights reserved. No part of this book shall be reproduced or transmitted in any form or by any means: electronic, mechanical, magnetic, photographic, including photocopying, recording, or by any information storage and retrieval system, or otherwise be copied for public or private use without prior written permission.

This book is a work of fiction. Names, characters, places, and incidents are products of the author's imagination or are used fictitiously. Any resemblance to actual events or locales, or any person, living or dead, is entirely coincidental.

Finicky Kitten

I asked, "Hey, silly finicky kitten.
Did you perhaps munch on my mitten?"
The kitten looked up at me and said,
"I merely gnawed your cabbage head."

"Ate a slice of watermelon minus seed
and two bites of jade garden weed."
"I chewed the spicy chicken in your pot,
but spit it back out, it was too hot."

"I licked some of your lemon mousse,
and finished off the roasted goose."
"I nibbled part of your luscious peach
with two oatmeal cookies I could reach."

"I gobbled goat cheese spread on bread
while crunching crackers in my bed."
"I chewed, but did not eat your old mitten,
because it was too inedible for this kitten."

Guardian Sphinx

Black guardian nestled on my pillow.
My protector from dark foreboding dreams.
I hear your purrs and heartbeat soft and low,
sleeps gentle guides that lead to mystic streams.

I peek at you. "What lies within your mind
small Sphinx, whose green eyes hold me in their spell?"
"Do you think I'm one of your furry kind?"
Your silent orbs mock me, but give no tell.

I close my eyes, and rest in sleep's soft arm.
Your paws reach out, caress my head with care,
but then you breathe and knead, this causes harm.
Your paws and breath leave mess within my hair.

I awake, feel your knots on my head,
and mutter, "Sphinx, would you just sleep in bed?"

My Pet Lizard

I have a pet, his name is Paul
who likes to crawl upon my wall,
then makes a leap onto my bed,
and falls asleep on my head.

I've filled his cage with sand
where he is king of the land,
and he lays upon his stone
in the sunlight all alone.

Sometimes he is hard to find
for he blends in with the blind
by changing color just like that
to match my pants, shirt, or hat.

My chameleon is first rate
even if he can't roller-skate,
and he is the best pet for me
to help scare all the girls I see.

Sly One

You act as if I'm the only one for you,
but I've seen you with quite a few.
You preen all day in the sun,
and smile at me while having fun.

You attack when I come down the hall,
and won't give me back my rubber ball.
You pretend you want to play,
then turn about and race away.

You take my shoes and use my bed,
and won't eat the food you're fed.
You seemed so serene when we met,
but you're a trickster cat, not my pet.

Breakfast By the Day

Monday's breakfast can only be
a bowl of Quaker oats for me.

Tuesday's breakfast is quite sublime,
I eat pancakes shaped like a dime.

Wednesday's breakfast I love the most,
scrambled eggs with jam and toast.

Thursday's breakfast is very quick,
pigs in a blanket on a stick.

Friday's breakfast is sure to please,
I get a quiche made just for me.

Saturday's breakfast is laidback,
biscuits, gravy, and bacon rack.

Sunday's breakfast can't be beat,
get up late and go out to eat.

Little Monkey

Monkey hanging from the tree,
would you like to play with me?
Monkey, Monkey by the gate,
can you come and roller-skate?
Monkey hopping on the log,
have you seen my little dog?
Monkey playing with the cat,
would you like to wear my hat?
Monkey, Monkey by the dam,
join me for bread and jam.

Monkey walking on the beach,
would you like to have a peach?
Monkey sitting by the sea,
will you jump the waves with me?
Monkey sailing on the boat,
would you like to ride my goat?
Monkey, Monkey in the tree,
stop tossing those seeds at me.
Monkey quit being a pest,
please lay down; it's time to rest.

The Closet

I opened the door, afraid of what I might find inside.
I reached up, turned on a light, when things began to fall.
Three baseball caps, a glove, top hat, then kid's slip-n-slide,
followed by a hockey stick, stuffed brown bear, and giant ball.

I fought to shut the door, but too late, a doll dropped on me,
a pile of sheets, horse blanket, and two old purple bags.
I found myself covered in old tee shirts and couldn't see,
I ripped them off in time to catch a large sack of dirty rags.

My foot slipped and I fell into the pile, wished they would stop,
but more things flew off the shelves, an Easter bunny, two hens,
a box of tissues, fluffy pink slippers, and red-striped top.
I thought that would be the last, but next came paper and pens.

I stood, heard a shelf break, screamed, and raced behind the door.
Heart pounding, I awoke tangled in blankets on the floor.

The Art of Wearing Glasses

I'm told sunglasses give you an allure.
So, slip on pink shades beneath straw hat.
I gaze in my mirror and feel demure,
yet somehow these glasses make me look fat.

Perhaps I need ones of a different hue,
silver, orange, purple or maybe light green.
No, a vibrant shade of metallic blue
notched with golden flecks to give eyes a sheen.

Yes, that is the way to go, bubbly blue
to tone down my size and make me seem small.
I'll be hidden, no one will have a clue
when I show up in glasses at the ball.

Ode to the Potato

How do I love thee? Let me count the ways.
I love thee fried, scalloped, mashed, or baked,
as pancakes, in a salad or stew, and chips by Lays
for you're the starch that binds me to my steak.

Your nutrients infuse my poor life and soul
with their rich potassium, fiber, and iron.
You are the vegetable on a plate, or in a bowl
that is more poetic than a poem by Byron.

You are the perfect food that I want to eat
each and every day for lunch or dinner.
No other vegetable with you can compete
for in truth, you are the ultimate winner.

Ode to Coffee

Your rich aroma wakes me up
each morning as I enjoy a cup.
Robust French-roast so strong,
you help to move my day along.

Flavored with a vanilla touch,
I find two cups is not enough.
At work another pot I fix,
now my cups number six.

Lunch comes and I can't resist,
two more cups have made my list.
Home at last from work to play,
I sip one more to end the day.

You look and taste extremely fine,
now my cups must number nine.
If there were only a coffee sea,
it would be heaven on earth for me.

Skunks are Not Kittens!

Of the fart squirrels beware,
lest they perfume the air.
Don't pet their little back,
or they just might attack.

If you're in the woods today,
let them go about their play.
If you see more than one,
It's best to turn around and run.

Sea Dragon

Once a dragon lived in the sea
with green fish scales who drank tea.
He'd chase sharks, or with dolphins play,
and terrorize ships every day.

He'd ride waves, or splash in the surf,
and leave his footprints in the turf.
At twilight when the sun would set,
he'd go sleep in a fishing net.

Circus Clowns' Delight

Inside circus tent at twilight
a band of clowns prance in and sing,
trip over feet to our delight.
We laugh at their pranks in the ring.

Fake flowers squirt, mock fight breaks out.
Then four clowns race in from the wing,
and toss water pails with a shout.
We laugh at their pranks in the ring.

Pies are next, and soon all are wet.
Two clowns climb pole and try to swing,
bar is missed, and they land in net.
We laugh at their pranks in the ring.

Inside circus tent at twilight,
we laugh at their pranks in the ring.

Luck—Good or Bad

Good Luck excelled at every game,
finding success and even fame.
Until he lost,
a bet that cost,
and claimed his brother was to blame.

Time for Ice Cream

The day was warm and sunny,
and piglet had some money.
So off he went to the store
after he finished his chore.

An ice cream cone sounded right
as a snack both cool and light.
Now, he sits out of the sun,
done with work, having fun.

Thoughts in the Meadow

Like a butterfly, I watch children play
a game of make believe beneath blue sky.
Their pure delight ignites my smile this day
like a butterfly.

I hear their joyous laughter rise on high,
chasing each other round and round today.
Childish enthusiasm makes me sigh.

Remembrance of my youth now gone away
when my siblings and I first sought to fly,
here amid lavender flowers one day
like a butterfly.

Dark and Stormy Night

One very dark and stormy night,
Shadow, my cat, runs in the door.
I head to bed, turn off the light.

Laughed at my cat, a pitiful sight
dripping water across the floor,
one very dark and stormy night.

Check to be sure the door is tight,
mop up the puddles, it's a chore.
I head to bed, turn off the light.

Lightning flickers silver bright
misses my boat upon the shore,
one very dark and stormy night.

Hear the cat howl as if in fright,
smack my toe and make it sore.
I head to bed, turn off the light.

Hope in the morning I can write
some poems that are not a bore.
One very dark and stormy night,
I head to bed, turn off the light.

Garden of Sunshine

I watch you sprout, children of gold,
around my house you spread your seeds.
Columns that soon my grass enfold,
and coax the earth to fill your needs.

Your tendril heads, bright waves of sun,
sway in the breeze, a churning sea.
Soft flaxen dots in green for fun,
you hem my house and old oak tree.

Yellow shoots that nod and smile on air,
a touch of sun in every field.
"What flower garden can compare?"
"Oh, dandelions to you, I yield."

Patience

Mom says patience will make me strong,
but why, oh why, does it take so long?

Farmer Andy's Family

I have a great family, said Andy
with a beautiful wife named Sandy,
two pigs and a dog,
three cats and a frog,
along with two goats make it dandy.

Kiss of Life

Once in a while, I would like a kiss
to keep my day from going amiss.
Sometimes, I need two or three,
other times, it takes more for me.

Sweet, light, and extremely fine,
kisses for me are quite sublime.
They make my day go much better
when dealing with the Irish setter.

If, I start my morning with just one,
nothing stops me till the setting sun.
Kisses were made for me to enjoy,
and I love them more than any boy.

Nothing in this world can ever compete
with a Hershey Kiss, life's special treat.

Lipstick on a Pig

Farmer Brown drove to the market in Knot,
with a load of pigs, he wanted to sell.
He touted his wares from a likely spot,
but lost his sales to a woman named Nell.

He thought a gimmick would do the trick.
So, he dressed a pig in tutu and hose.
A wig of red hair to match her lipstick,
and eyelashes curling down to her nose.

A tune he began to play on his flute,
as the pig danced around doing a jig.
The people laughed at its antics so cute,
that each decided they must buy a pig.

His wares quickly sold, faster than honey,
except for the one, who he named Money.

Too Many Pets

I'm late for work, my tire is flat;
It doesn't matter, just feed the cat.

The baby's crying, there's a clog in the sink;
Just keep on moving and brush the mink.

My clothes don't fit, the kids won't rake;
Don't think about it, just find the snake.

The dinner's burnt, but I don't care;
For now, it's time to comb the mare.

Put the kids to bed, so I can jog;
Then go outside and wash the hog.

The day is done, the sun has set;
Thank God, I don't have another pet.

Napkin—Friend or Foe?

Napkin, napkin by my plate,
why'd you wipe off what I ate?

From my hands and my face,
scrubbing every little trace.

No milk or sauce left on me,
nor a speck of grease to see.

Cleaned me up, made me shine,
but I liked that grime of mine.

Little Terror

I have a small terrier named Robby
who chews my books for a hobby.
He's eaten my drapes,
as if they were grapes,
and now I'm replacing my lobby.

23

The Owl & the Pussycat Revised

The Owl and the Pussycat went into space,
In a modified Jupiter C.
They took some lox and standard clocks;
And an ape with a Ph.D.
The Owl took a sight on the stars above,
And sang to the guide beam's sound.
"Oh, lovely Pussy, Oh Pussy my love,
We should never have left the ground,
The ground, the ground!
We should never have left the ground."

Pussy said to the Owl, "Our atmosphere's foul,
And your singing upsetting our course.
But let us be wedded, and compute where we're headed;
We'll send our decision in Morse."
So, they rocketed gay the elliptical way,
To the land where the fungus grows.
And there as he should a Martian stood,
On a ring instead of his toes,
His toes, his toes,
On a ring instead of his toes.

"Will you loan us your ring, if the Owl doesn't sing?"
Telepathed back the Martian, "I will."
So, they dragged it away, and were married next day,
By some sort of a thing with a gill.
They dined on yams, and boneless hams,
While the Martian espied them in mirth.
And hand in hand on the ruddy sand,
Each thumbed his nose at the earth,
The earth, the earth,
Each thumbed his nose at the earth.

Where is My Pot of Luck?

A wee leprechaun named O'Shay
misplaced his pot of luck one day.
He searched the closets in each room,
and swept his cottage with a broom.
He found a monkey, bat, and truck,
but did not find his pot of luck.

He went outside, searched his wagon,
waking up a sleeping dragon.
He checked the barn and cellar too,
found four hens and a cockatoo.
Also, a sheep, a goat and duck,
but did not find his pot of luck.

So off he went to search the trees,
but all he found were honeybees.
Then taking a path to the lake,
he spied two hares, a frog and snake.
Near shore he found a stately buck,
but did not find his pot of luck.

The day turned dark, a storm blew in,
raindrops soon soaked him to the skin.
He raced for home quick as could be
on ground turned to a muddy sea.
He tripped on something in the muck,
and there he found his pot of luck.

Green Beer with Ham

I do not like green beer with ham.
"It's just not Irish," grumbled Sam.
I will not drink it on a boat.
I will not drink it with a goat.

I do not like green beer with ham.
"It's just not Irish," grumbled Sam.
I will not drink it with a mouse.
I will not drink it in my house.

I do not like green beer with ham.
"It's just not Irish," grumbled Sam.
I will not drink it with a mare.
I will not drink it on a dare.

I do not like green beer with ham.
"It's just not Irish," grumbled Sam.
I will not drink it with an egg.
I will not drink it from a keg.

I do not like green beer with ham.
"It's just not Irish," grumbled Sam.
I will not drink it, not one sip.
No green beer will touch my lip.

I do not want green in my beer
to give a Happy St. Pat's cheer.
I do not like green beer with ham.
"It's just not Irish," grumbled Sam.

Back in the Good Old Days

Oh, if only we could slide backward in time
to those olden days when coke was a dime.
Where fins were the latest style on each car,
and we'd catch lightning bugs in a mason jar.

We'd spend weekends with picnics in the park,
and no one feared going out after dark.
Our music came on black vinyl not CD,
and we spent evenings with a book to read.

On summer days we loved an ice cream bar
while at the drive-in movies in our car.
Every clerk would count change at the store,
and milk was delivered to our front door.

We'd play hide and seek in our yard outside,
and on Sundays we'd all go for a ride.
Then play checkers, baseball, or kick the can,
and our air conditioning was an old box fan.

Life was less stressful, a slower pace and age,
then the world evolved, turned another page.
Now technology has come to change our ways,
yet we recall with fondness those olden days.

Green is the Color I'll Wear

I'm going green in what I wear today,
don't feel like being a yellow sunray,
or walking about in that deep blue sea,
those colors don't do a thing for me.

The days are past when I might dress in black.
I've put those Goth clothes back on the rack,
and I've no need to garb myself in red,
it's a color for vampires whom I dread.

Orange is just so wild, too bubbly and bold,
and purple, well they say it's for the old.
I'd wear brown, but it's too drab for today,
and gray is best worn on a rainy day.

Perhaps white would suffice, so ghostly pale.
No, I'd appear dead, not hearty and hale.
So, wearing green is what it has to be,
and now I'm a vibrant leaf on a tree.

Tale of Two Socks

Two socks went in the washer.
A pair, a matching set.
Yet, when I took the clothes out,
only one was left.

Grandpa's Suspenders

My grandpa wore striped suspenders
every day to hold up his pants.
He would stretch them out with his hands
when making a point, or with rants.

Grandpa said they had many uses
such as helping you climb a tree,
or corralling a two-year old
buzzing 'round the porch like a bee.

He said they made a neat slingshot,
and were better than any belt.
They worked great to carry in wood,
or bag of ice, so it didn't melt.

My Grandpa loved his suspenders,
and all us kids thought they were cool.
So, he gave each of us a pair
which we wore every day to school.

Windchime on My Porch

A dragon whispers on the summer breeze,
a silhouette that chimes with all its might.
As velvet winds ripple its scales with ease,
a dragon whispers on the summer breeze.
Soft musical notes it sends forth to please
from the flicker of dawn till dark of night.
A dragon whispers on the summer breeze,
a silhouette that chimes with all its might.

Rainy Day

I sit and watch spring raindrops fall
while grey cat sleeps on windowsill.
Two kids splash puddles against wall
on my house near the village mill.

I sense a poem that I must write,
and scratch on paper with a quill.
The tinkle of rain changes its might
on my house near the village mill.

Hear thunder's loud crash, a freight train
sound echoes cross willow hill.
Poor oak leaves droop from pouring rain
on my house near the village mill.

I sit and watch spring raindrops fall
on my house near the village mill.

My Furry Inkblot

A furry drop of midnight sky,
inkblot pressed against windowsill.
She mews, a gentle little cry,
and claws at glass with a will.

Outside she sees red bird in flight,
body pivots, jumps down to floor.
Her green eyes gleam with eerie light,
races about, scratches at the door.

I open door, she bounds cross snow,
an inky blot mid cotton cloud.
Red bird takes flight, she sadly knows
her prey is lost, she mews aloud.

I Refuse to Age

I see no point in growing old,
or worry what to do each day.
Instead, I work at being bold,
go swimming in the local bay.

My way of life leads me to say,
I see no point in growing old.
Instead, I paint and sculpt in clay,
or take a trip to mine for gold.

I do not feel the days grow cold
as winter seeks to come my way.
I see no point in growing old,
or watch my youth fade away.

I live what age I choose today,
this hand of time I will not fold.
Until the end takes me one day,
I see no point in growing old.

Sanctuary

Within the glen a fairy ring
and there the child did lie.
She heard the fairies sing
beneath a moonlit sky.

Safe from the hunter's rage,
she slept peaceful in the dark.
Morning came, turned a page,
the child awoke; a lark.

Spring's in the Air

I walk in the meadow among new heather,
feel the touch of a zephyr in my hair.
I embrace return of warm spring's weather,
and inhale scent of bluebells on the air.
I stroll through fields of golden daffodils,
sit on velvet grass beneath oak trees.
I amble along path towards the hills,
watch playful monarch, and two busy bees.
Now winter snows have become crystal stream,
and new sprouts appear, green covers the earth.
I can walk woodland paths, no longer dream
of waiting for spring to come with its mirth.
For winter has shed its skin, the land glows,
a painter's canvas where a warm wind blows.

Rose in the Wall

A yellow rose wound gently through the wall
into the meadow for a different view,
it felt the early stage of autumn call.
A yellow rose wound gently through the wall,
and saw the maple leaves decked out for fall,
sighed deeply, wished that it could change its hue.
A yellow rose wound gently through the wall
into the meadow for a different view.

Within Oak Groves

Step within oak groves
where magic dreams,
and dragons reside.
Here tree frogs sing,
beneath golden moons,
and fairies dance
mid mushroom rings.

Oak spirits converse
in midnight's hour
beside cerulean streams,
amuse primrose and pine
with old tales of wizards
from their youth till sleep
comes with magic dreams.

Child of Three

I saw three-year-old's one day,
a rainbow mix of color at play.
Racing about without a care,
laughing as wind blew their hair.

Yet on my walk around the town,
people spat hate, it made me frown.
Black yelled at white, young at old,
such loathing, made my soul cold.

Where did people learn this trait?
Children have to be taught to hate.
It would be better if each one could be
turned back into a child of three.

My Little Pup

Why does my dog bark when I clean?
Yips and yaps as I walk around.
She sounds ferocious and so mean,
you'd think she was an old coon hound.

Instead, she's just a Yorkie pup,
minute in stature, black and Tan.
She only wants to be picked up,
and slowly melt into my hand.

Avian Troubadour

Cardinal hides within branches,
a speck of scarlet out of sight.
Tiny avian troubadour
sings a song for me with delight.

Beneath a cloudless azure sky,
his tune speaks sadness and of light.
I listen to his melody,
and feel my soul soar off in flight.

Fairy Patio Umbrella

A minute ivory mushroom
sprouts within scraggly old oak tree.
Fairies' patio umbrella,
a shade from rays and busy bee.

Fairies stay dry beneath its lip,
safe from murky sky's pouring rain.
A tiny haven where they sit,
and nibble their meal made from grain.

Eventide comes, the night turns dark,
and the fairies soon go to sleep.
Content beneath their outdoor shade
while all around the tree frogs cheep.

Autumn Arrives

Now Summer ends with a cool breeze.
Here comes Autumn with amber leaves.
The crickets chirp their final song,
know Jack Frost's coming won't be long.
Flame bright pumpkins laugh in the patch
waiting for Harvest Moon to hatch.

Oaks and maples turn gold and red,
costumes for the fall ball ahead.
The wind whispers to all the trees,
"It's time to let me have your leaves
to dance and swirl in autumn flight
beneath a starry moonlit night."

Scarecrows pop up in cornfield rows,
sit on porches with festive bows.
The squirrels store acorns in their trees,
and footsteps crinkle through the leaves.
Chilled air brings need for fall attire,
and cup of cider by the fire.

Turning of the Leaves

The jade leaves turn and fall away,
tearful rivulets from maple trees.
Leaf cycle brings each a new hue,
exhibits Jack Frost's color sprees.

Autumn paints the world merrily
with joy and laughter for each day.
Leaves enjoy their masquerade ball,
dance with cool winds along their way.

Cat Angel

Tabby frolics in winter white,
creates an angel in the snow.
Enjoys day beneath golden light,
her body stretches like a bow.

A furry child without a care,
wiggles mid snowflake covered ground.
Leaves her imprint with world to share,
and then sprints off without a sound.

Pillow Fight

The pillow and I had a fight
while I slept on it last night.

Stuffed too full, I threw it about,
ripped and tore its fluffing out.

Deflated now, inners in a heap,
means I can get back to sleep.

Cold Day

I peak through the green window sash,
see ground covered in snowy trash.
The cold wind howls, caresses house,
watch my blanket move, spy the mouse.

The temperature is only three,
my water dish, a frozen sea.
Think I will just call it a day,
sneak under blanket, there I'll stay.

Cuteness Monster

She had twin eyes of liquid green,
the prettiest I'd ever seen.
Wore a jade scaled armor cloak,
loved to take a four-hour soak.

She had a silver shell on back
protection from a sneak attack.
Webbed feet, and shell upon her tail,
looked innocent but was not frail.

Leaf Ball

There once was a man named Jake
who taught two squirrels to rake.
So now in the fall
they make a leaf ball
and roll it down to the lake.

Chocolate Disaster

Early one morning, I started to bake
a seven-layer chocolate fudge cake.
I mixed it up and poured it into pans,
put it in the oven and called my nans.

Got the scoop on staking, how long to cool,
then got my new book and sat on a stool.
I took the pans out when the timer rang,
set them to cool, fixed fudge icing with Tang.

Ready now, I iced each layer with glee,
stacked high on a plate for the gang to see.
Finished, I picked it up, opened the fridge door,
next thing I knew, it splattered on the floor.

The icing coated the door and inside,
and the cake on the floor leaned to one side.
The moral of this story, I should bake
nothing larger than a one-layer cake.

Life's A Garden—Dig It!

Spring has sprung, time to dig
feel dirt between your toes.
Plant flowers, or new tree
to shade you from your woes.

Watch garden spring alive,
sprout buds of gold and red.
Just remember to keep
your old dog out of the bed.

The Tree Frog Sang

I saw a tree frog on the ground
with gray and white spots all around.
It hopped about, jumped on a log,
gave a strange look at my hound dog.
Then the tree frog sang.

Its croak was crisp amid the song,
and made me want to sing along.
Join its tune about birds and bees,
or autumn leaves from old oak trees.
That the tree frog sang.

Its melody danced with the breeze
in sadness for the coming freeze.
My heart entwined its song that day.
I let it carry me away.
To where the tree frog sang.

Silly Kitty

My tongue is a marvelous tool.
See I can touch my nose, so cool.
I use it to clean paws and head,
and sometimes lick things that are dead.

I stick it out, drool on your lace,
then lick your hand and clean your face.
You laugh, say silly cat mid squirms.
Race off, wash up, and scream "Cat Germs."

Tabby and the Vinyl Blinds

A small tabby kitten wanted to see
what was outside her window on the tree.
From the couch she jumped to windowsill,
but blinds were in the way, she took a spill.

Now caught in vinyl by belly she hangs,
disgustingly meowing bearing her fangs.
She calls for a human to set her free,
but will have to wait, no one is home till three.

Autumn Fae

The golden Autumn Fae
with wand has come today.
She tiptoes up oak tree
to set its gold leaves free.
They glide on sky of blue
in new bright shades of hue.

She wanders round the glen
not seen by eyes of men.
She leaves behind her gift
to sparkle and uplift.
Colored leaves dance their ball
thanks to the Fae of Fall.

Sidewalk Ends

So, we came to where the sidewalk ends,
and there we found tiny fairy friends
within the bushes just pass the sign
who invited us with them to dine.

So, we spent some time, an hour or three,
and found they were just like you and me.
Then the sky was painted in black night,
and they sent us home with fairy light.

Tale Of Eight Little Pumpkins

Eight little pumpkins sitting on a log,
One gets up to walk the dog.
Seven little pumpkins now remain,
One wanders off to catch a train.
Six little pumpkins all in a row,
One goes shopping to buy a bow.
Five little pumpkins discover a nest,
One walks home to get some rest.
Four little pumpkins stroll by the sea,
One goes sailing, now there are three.
Three little pumpkins climb on rocks,
One runs home to darn its socks.
Two little pumpkins playing with a duck,
One races down the lane after a truck.
One little pumpkin waits by the gate,
A Jack-O-Lantern is its fate.

Smashed Jack

Alas poor Jack, I knew him well.
As a pumpkin, he was quite swell.
A lantern he wanted to be,
not a simple pumpkin like me.
In youth he grew, became quite round,
the largest pumpkin from our ground.
Jack was carved, and set out at night,
looking fine with his shiny light.
Then fate stepped in to have its say,
Jack was smashed on Halloween day.
No longer an orange lantern round.
In pieces, he lies on the ground.

Jack-O-Tater

While Jack-O-Lanterns are quite nice,
some people can't afford the price
to purchase pumpkins, and then make
a scary face, or brain that's fake.
So, potatoes are what you use
to crave your scary face, or two.
Then set them on your porch with glee
displayed for all the world to see.

Jack-O-Lanterns Go Marching

Jack-O-Lanterns go marching one by one,
the little one's head bangs his drum.
Jack-O-Lanterns go marching two by two,
the little one trips over his clown shoe.
Jack-O-Lanterns go marching three by three,
the little one flings paper on a tree.
Jack-o-lanterns go marching four by four,
the little one spray paints a door.
Jack-O-Lanterns go marching five by five,
the little one starts singing jive.
Jack-O-Lanterns go marching six by six,
the little one beats a piñata with a stick.
Jack-O-Lanterns go marching seven by seven,
the little one stops at Pizza Heaven.
Jack-O-Lanterns go marching eight by eight,
the little one breaks down the gate.
Jack-O-Lanterns go marching nine by nine,
the little one says it's time to dine.
Jack-O-Lanterns go marching ten by ten,
the little one says let's sleep in the pen.

What Lies Under My Bed?

At night, when I lay down my sleepy head,
my mind wonders, "What lies under my bed?"
Are monsters waiting to disturb my sleep?
Perhaps white carnivorous fluffy sheep,
or mammoth wide mouth frogs with razor fangs
whose ultimate sweet is children with bangs.
I cower afraid, and filled with such dread
that monsters really live under my bed.
It's just my imagination, I think,
then something rattles, and I hear a clink.
I gaze down, see dark move, a scurrying rat.
I scream, ball of fur attacks. It's my cat.

Lions on Conner Street

Leo and Randall are their names,
and they love to play dress-up games.
In front of a grey house these lions sit,
decked out each month in a new outfit
Chiseled stone figures that display their flair
cloaked in unique hats, clothes and hair.

The lions bring a smile to everyone's lips
while passing by on their road trips.
Each month new themes the lions display,
leaving us to wonder what outfit they'll wear next day.
These lions bring joy with their dress,
and help us to relieve our stress.

Elf on the Shelf

Once I had a miniature elf
who enjoyed sitting on a shelf,
or I'd find him reading my book
on the table in breakfast nook.

Sometimes he'd hide in my bathtub,
surprise me when I went to scrub.
Or pop out from behind a broom,
and chase my cat around the room.

He wore a suit of candy red
with pointed shoes and cap on head.
His face was painted with a grin
as he leaned against my cup of tin.

That elf could move around my house
sneakier than a ghostly mouse.
Yet, I always found him at night
resting against my bedroom light.

Santa's Helper

My name is Elfie Paws,
and I help Santa Claus.
Though my hat doesn't fit,
I still deliver gifts.

With bells on my collar
I come when he hollers.
Take a ride on his sleigh,
I'm his helper each day.

With a smile on my face,
I keep up with his pace.
For my work, I get a ball.
So, Merry Christmas all.

Mary A. Couch, an Administrative Assistant for Taylored Systems LLC, a technology company in Noblesville, learned the art of poetry from her mother and two grandmothers who were storytellers and artists. She enjoys writing poems showing her Celtic heritage by revealing the spirits that live in nature and the oneness of the universe. Her poems have been published in a variety of venues including *Poetic Nature in the Hoosierland, Twin Muses: Art & Poetry, An Evening with the Writing Muse, Polk Street Review, Encore, Pegasus, Poetry and Paint,* and *Last Stanza Poetry Journal.* She is a published author of three books: *Hoosier Haiku: Poetic Snippets from the Heartland, Hoosier WordArt: Communing with the Chippewa,* and *Hoosier WordArt: Generations.* She and her mother, Alice B. Couch, also published a chapbook called *Two Views.* She is a past Premier Poet for the Poetry Society of Indiana.

www.ingramcontent.com/pod-product-compliance
Lightning Source LLC
Chambersburg PA
CBHW070318160726
47999CB00003B/1069